this is ~~history~~

HerStory

a celebration of
remarkable women
who changed the world

harriet dyer

summersdale

THIS IS HERSTORY

An Hachette UK Company
www.hachette.co.uk

Summersdale Publishers Ltd
Part of Octopus Publishing Group Limited
Carmelite House
50 Victoria Embankment
LONDON
EC4Y 0DZ
UK

www.summersdale.com

Printed and bound in Malta

ISBN: 978-1-78685-822-1

Substantial discounts on bulk quantities of Summersdale books are available to corporations, professional associations and other organisations. For details contact general enquiries: telephone: +44 (0) 1243 771107 or email: enquiries@summersdale.com.

Contents

Introduction

Women are makers of history, but you might struggle to find their stories in a lot of books. A worthy wife here, a famous beauty there, but very rarely a pioneering figure. Virginia Woolf wrote her career-defining work *A Room of One's Own* after performing this very exercise and finding her results wanting.

There is no doubt that, for centuries, women have had almost every obstacle placed in their path: lack of education, laws restricting their rights, laws that defined them as property, and social stigma placed on any woman who dared to step off her preordained path. Yet, if you look a bit closer at history, you'll start to see women where you didn't before.

So, why do we not know their stories? Some women have been deliberately obliterated by their enemies and even their friends. For instance, it is thought that the name of Hatshepsut – Egypt's second female pharaoh and one of its greatest – was scrubbed from temple walls by her own grandson, Amenhotep II. Others have been slandered posthumously. Catherine II, one of Russia's most renowned rulers, is chiefly known in popular culture for having sex with horses. This seems to be a kind of schoolyard rumour that even respected historians, for some reason, enjoy repeating – a rumour which probably only arose as a result of her enjoying a string of lovers. Certainly, many kings have had a poorer historical reputation and a higher number of lovers, yet are not smeared by similar comments. Others, it seems, just drop out of the history books. It is not clear why Frida Kahlo, who was successful in her own lifetime, has only recently become well known, and was even excluded from the *Oxford Concise Dictionary of Artists* until 1990.

And there are countless more. Did you know the first recorded poet in the world was a priestess named Enheduanna? Have you heard of Ching Shih, the most successful pirate in history, who commanded a feared navy of 70,000 pirates? Were you aware that the technology on which Wi-Fi – the basis of modern life as we know it – was developed by Hedy Lamarr, the Hollywood actress?

Today, we are hungry for women's stories and we refuse to accept that they don't exist. We are peeling back the dusty layers of our history books and seeing the women that were there all along: the great, the good, the mighty, the genius, the formidable – and many more. So read on and find all the herstory you've missed.

"

faithful woman exceeding in wisdom

opens [her] mouth [to recite] over cooled lined tablets

always consults lapis tablets

[and] gives strong council to all lands.

ENHEDUANNA

2285–50 BC

High priestess and the first named poet in history.

"

Hatshepsut

Dates: 1507–1458 BC
Country of origin: Egypt

Longest-reigning female Pharaoh of Egypt, who commissioned many landmarks that still stand today including the Temple of Hatshepsut

During her rule, Hatshepsut ordered the construction of many temples, statues and monuments, including the beautiful Temple of Hatshepsut which is still standing today. She had them inscribed with her achievements and records of her divine birth and kingship (ancient Egypt had no Queen role). However, some decades after her reign, most of her statues were pulled down and her name was scratched off many carvings in a still-unexplained attempt to erase her rule. Hatshepsut took the throne as regent for her husband's son, Thutmose III, but soon seized power in her own right, reigning for around 21 years. Her rule was largely peaceful, marked by successful trading expeditions and hundreds of grand construction projects. Her expedition to Punt saw the first recorded attempt to import foreign trees; her emissaries returned with 31 myrrh trees, whereupon they were planted in the courtyard of her great temple.

Sappho

Dates: *c.*620–570 BC
Country of origin: Greece

> *Hugely influential poet and possible inventor of the plectrum*

Not much is known of Sappho's life: she was born to a wealthy family on Lesbos in 630 BC and was probably married. Even her poetry, supposed to once number around 10,000 lines, only survives in fragments, with just one complete poem still existing. However, in her lifetime, she was astonishingly successful and her poetry was influential for nearly a thousand years after her death. Plato referred to her as the 'tenth muse' and she was considered one of the nine 'canonical lyric poets of Ancient Greece' – meaning she was an essential part of any comprehensive Ancient Greek literary education. A vase portraying Sappho strumming a lyre is the first known depiction of a plectrum, leading some to speculate she invented it. The subjects of her poetry were many but she is most famous for her erotic writing about women. The words 'sapphic' and 'lesbian' derive respectively from her name and her place of birth.

We are also the only ones who give birth to men.

GORGO OF SPARTA, ON BEING ASKED WHY SPARTAN WOMEN WERE THE ONLY PEOPLE WHO CAN RULE MEN.

c.480 BC
Queen of Sparta, wife of Leonidas I, known for her judgement and political advice.

Boudica

Dates: *c*.30–61
Country of origin: Britain

Leader of the Iceni tribe who revolted against the Roman Empire

When Boudica's husband, Prasutagus, King of the Iceni, died, he left his kingdom to be ruled equally by his two daughters and the Roman emperor. The Roman centurions in Britain ignored this and not only annexed his land but ordered Boudica to be flogged and her daughters raped. Boudica rose up and led the Iceni tribe in rebellion, intending to drive the Romans out of Britain. The Roman generals expected to easily defeat her but Boudica defeated the first small, under-armed force that the Romans sent to meet them, and then a second. The Iceni gathered momentum, sweeping through England and destroying settlements, including what was then known as Londinium (now London). Iceni women and men fought together and around 80,000 Romans and Britons were killed and mutilated. Finally, Boudica's large army met the governor of Britain's smaller but better-trained army and were defeated. Reports on the fate of Boudica differ: some say she took her own life while others say she fell sick and died.

JOIN THE MALE AND THE FEMALE, AND YOU WILL FIND WHAT IS SOUGHT.

MARY THE PROPHETESS,
ON THE ATTRACTION OF OPPOSITES

*c.*100 AD

Credited as the first alchemist of the Western
world and supposed inventor of the *bain-marie*, among other chemical apparatus.

Hypatia

Dates: *c.*350–415
Country of origin: Egypt

Renowned philosopher, astronomer and mathematician

A respected teacher and academic at the University of Alexandria, Hypatia was considered one of the brightest minds of her time. In a letter to a friend, one of her pupils described her as 'a person so renowned, her reputation seemed literally incredible'. Unfortunately, little of her work has survived the millennia, although we do know that she wrote commentaries on mathematical theories of the time, constructed machines with which to measure the stars and gave lectures on writing and philosophy. Popular and well-respected, Hypatia was politically influential. However, Christian bishop Cyril considered her a thorn in his side, not just because she was Neoplatonic but because she was a woman too. Her life was cut short when a mob, possibly incited by Cyril, seized her and brutally murdered her.

'Reserve your right to think, for even to think wrongly is better than not to think at all.'

May I never see the day when those who meet me do not call me Empress.

EMPRESS THEODORA OF BYZANTINIUM

497–548 AD

Daughter of a bear-trainer, Theodora rose to rule the Byzantine Empire with her husband Justinian I. She instituted laws that forbade forced prostitution and the killing of adulterous wives and was posthumously made a Christian saint.

Seondeok of Silla

Dates: *c.*595–647
Country of origin: Silla (now part of South Korea)

First female ruler of Silla and second female ruler recorded in East Asian history

Princess Deokman always knew she wanted to be a leader. When her father, the king of Silla, decided to bequeath his kingdom to his son-in-law, Deokman pleaded with him to give her the opportunity to rule. He agreed on the condition that Deokman would compete for the throne and win the support of her people. She succeeded, and in January AD 632 was crowned Queen Seondeok of Silla. Her rule heralded a golden age of literature and the arts, and she oversaw the building of many great monuments, some of which still stand today. Among them are Cheomseongdae, the oldest observatory in East Asia, and the temple of Hwangnyongsa, for which she commissioned an impressive 80-metre-tall pagoda, making the temple the tallest structure in East Asia at the time.

Olga of Kiev

Dates: *c.*890–969
Country of origin: Kiev

Successful ruler, orchestrator of revenge and Christian saint

When Olga's husband, Igor of Kiev, died in AD 945, she became regent for their three-year-old son Svyatoslav. She ruled successfully in his name for around 15 years, handing over the kingdom of Kiev when he came of age but ruling it during his long absences for military campaigns. However, Olga's hold on power stemmed from a burning desire for revenge.

Igor was murdered when visiting the Drevelians to collect a tithe. After her husband's death, the Drevelians sent 20 envoys to Olga, hoping to persuade her to marry their prince. She had them buried alive and sent word to the Drevelians that she accepted their proposal, asking for their finest officials to come and celebrate her marriage. Upon their arrival, she had them killed too. Olga sent further word to the Drevelians, requesting that thousands of them attend a funeral feast for her husband. Apparently still suspecting nothing, they accepted. Olga's soldiers killed them all. Finally, she burned down their city. Despite this, by most accounts in the years that followed, Olga was a progressive ruler; her reign was marked by legal reform and after her death she was made a Christian saint for spreading Christianity to her country.

"

We ought to love even those who hate us.

MURASAKI SHIKIBU

*c.*978–1025

Japanese lady-in-waiting and author of the world's first novel, *The Tale of Genji.*

"

By the wrath of God, queen of England.

ELEANOR OF AQUITAINE'S SIGNATURE

1122–1204

Divorced King Louis VII of France in order to marry King Henry II of England. She was a formidable player in English and international politics during her 83 years, even leading the Second Crusade.

7

Tamar of Georgia

Dates: *c.*1160–1213
Country of origin: Georgia

Remembered as Tamar the Great, she oversaw a golden age in Georgian history

Tamar first came to power in 1178, when she was named co-ruler by her father George III. Then, in 1184, she ruled as queen regnant. During her rule, Tamar crushed several attempted coups, including two from her ex-husband, and oversaw the greatest expansion of the Georgian kingdom in history. She came to be known as 'King of Kings and Queen of Queens of the Abkhazians, Kartvelians, Arranians, Kakhetians, and Armenians'. So great was her wealth from the spoils of war, it was said that in Georgia 'the peasants were like nobles, the nobles like princes, and the princes like kings.' Of Tamar herself, her father described her best when he said 'One knows a lion by its claws and Tamar by her actions.'

YOU AND I
HAVE SO MUCH LOVE
THAT IT
BURNS LIKE A FIRE
IN WHICH WE BAKE A LUMP OF CLAY
MOULDED INTO A FIGURE OF YOU
AND A FIGURE OF ME.

GUAN DAOSHENG

1262–1319

Famous Chinese bamboo painter
who included poems in her art.

Joan of Arc

Dates: 1412–31
Country of origin: France

> Led the French army in several victories against the powerful English army

As a child, Joan saw visions of long-dead Christian saints who, she claimed, told her she must help France in their ongoing war against England. She demanded an armed escort to take her to the French court where she could help her king. Surprisingly, she got it, and in an even more unlikely turn of events, Charles VII of France gave her permission to lead his army. Soon most French citizens believed Joan to be led by God. Her inspirational leadership resulted in victory after years of defeat. Joan and her family were ennobled by Charles in thanks. However, her success did not last. Joan was pulled from her horse while attacking an enemy camp and she was captured by English allies. She was executed after an unfair trial for the charges of heresy and crossdressing. Joan is now remembered as a national hero and a saint.

'I must be at the King's side… there will be no help (for the kingdom) if not from me.'

All actions have evolved
from the taste of flight;
the hope of freedom
moves our cells
and limbs.

MEERA

1498–1546

Indian Hindi mystic poet. Her poetry
and religious passion was frowned upon at
the time as unbecoming to a princess, but
she is remembered as one of India's
most famous poets and celebrated
in places as a saint.

Elizabeth I of England

Dates: 1533–1603
Country of origin: England

Remembered as one of England's greatest rulers

The daughter of an executed mother and a king obsessed with producing a male heir, Elizabeth was an unlikely candidate for the English throne. Only the second queen of England, she ruled for 44 prosperous and mostly peaceful years – and this was no mean feat given that when she inherited the crown it was in debt. Her reign was marked by great exploration to lands including the 'New World' (the Americas), her patronage to writers, poets and dramatists, including William Shakespeare, and the wealth she amassed for the crown. During her rule, England was considered unparalleled in Europe in terms of its money and power. Elizabeth herself lived a storied life, from being held captive in the Tower of London during the reign of her sister Mary I to her refusal to marry and share the power of the crown with a man.

'I have the body of a weak, feeble woman;
but I have the heart and stomach of a king,
and of a King of England too.'

> **The virtue of man and virtue of woman are the same thing, since God bestowed on them the same creation and the same honour.**

MARIE DE GOURNAY

1565–1645

French writer and author of *The Equality of Men and Women*, a defence of women's rights including the right to be educated.

I had a taste for roving and seeing the world.

CATALINA DE ERAUSO

1592–1650

Former nun who disguised herself as a man, rising to the rank of second lieutenant in the Spanish army. A brawler, thief and seducer of women, who was constantly escaping arrest.

A MAID MAY BE A SCHOLAR.

ANNA MARIA VAN SCHURMAN

1607–78

Dutch painter, poet and scholar, who was the first woman to study at a Dutch university. She was an early defender of women's rights in the Western world.

Artemisia Gentileschi

Dates: 1593–1652/3
Country of origin: Italy

Baroque painter, celebrated in her lifetime and now considered to be one of the greatest painters of her time

During a time when it was uncommon for a woman to be a commercially successful artist, Artemisia was celebrated as a skilled painter and a master of colour and construction. She was famed for her studies of Biblical heroines and her work was admired by many, including Charles I of England and Philip IV of Spain. Her unlikely career was nearly stopped before it began when she participated in the trial of the man who raped her. She was questioned and tortured with thumbscrews but held true to her story; her attacker was imprisoned and sentenced to exile, although the sentence was later lifted. Exposure to public scrutiny on that level often ruined women of the time, but Artemisia persevered and became one of the greatest painters of the period. In addition to her striking use of colour and technical ability, she painted her heroines with a depth of emotion and inner life that was uncommon for the time. By the end of her life, Artemisia was the head of a large studio with many apprentices – an achievement for any painter of the time but especially so for a female painter.

'As long as I live, I will have control over my being. My illustrious lordship, I'll show you what a woman can do.'

In Nature, we have
as clear an understanding
as men, if we were bred in
Schools to Mature our Brains.

MARGARET CAVENDISH ON WOMEN

1623–76

English poet, philosopher, science
essayist and writer. Authored an
early science-fiction novel,
The Blazing World.

Aphra Behn

Dates: 1640–89
Country of origin: England

Royalist, spy and groundbreaking playwright

Aphra Behn's life consisted of multiple acts – perhaps appropriate for one who would become one of England's foremost playwrights. Her childhood years aren't well documented – possibly as a result of her later efforts to obscure her origins – but a few years before the start of the English Civil War, she travelled outside of England. Soon after the monarchy was restored to England, she came to the attention of Charles II, who commissioned her as a spy and sent her to Holland. She was embedded in Amsterdam and fed important information back to her country, but it was not financially rewarding work; Aphra spent a short time in a debtors' prison before the British government paid her debts. Aphra took up writing plays, becoming famed for her Restoration comedies. These plays largely focused on the previously exiled British Royalist court and are now used as a window into the privileged and libertine morals of Charles II's 'Merry Monarch' reign. Unusually for a woman of the time, Aphra earned her living by writing. She was one of the first English women to do so.

They tell us we mistake our sex and way;

Good breeding, fashion, dancing,
dressing, play

Are the accomplishments we
should desire;

To write, or read, or think, or to inquire

Would cloud our beauty, and
exhaust our time,

And interrupt the conquests of our prime;

Whilst the dull manage of a servile house

Is held by some our outmost art, and use.

ANNE FINCH

1661–1720

English aristocratic poet known for her writing
in a time when few women wrote.

But you, tho you understand nothing of it, pretend to teach us an Art much more difficult (And which ought to be kept a Secret amongst Women as much as is possible).

ELIZABETH CELLIER TO A DOCTOR DECRYING FEMALE MIDWIVES AND THEIR SKILLS

*c.*1668

Popish pamphleteer and midwife, who first campaigned to displace the Stuart monarchy and then to argue for the rights and unionisation of midwives.

Julie d'Aubigny

Dates: *c.*1670–1707
Country of origin: France

Professional opera singer, talented duellist, adventurer and lover of men and women

Much of what is known of Julie d'Aubigny is considered to be apocryphal but if even half of the stories about her are true, oh what a woman she was! An expert fencer, on-and-off opera star and lover of both men and women, Julie was passionate and adventurous. Perhaps the most famous episode of her life is one from her youth when, upon discovering her affair with a young lady, the woman's parents sent Julie's lover to a nunnery. Undeterred, she joined the convent herself and rescued her love, although she was charged with kidnapping, body snatching and arson in the process. Later in her life she publicly kissed an attractive noblewoman at a ball, so enraging three aristocrats that they each challenged her to a duel. She defeated them all and returned to the party, later fleeing to Brussels to lie low (enjoying an affair with a German prince while she was there).

PAINTING AND LIVING HAVE ALWAYS BEEN ONE AND THE SAME THING FOR ME.

ÉLISABETH VIGÉE LE BRUN

1755–1842

French eighteenth-century society portrait painter
and official portrait painter of Marie Antoinette.

Elizabeth of Russia

Dates: 1709–62
Country of origin: Russia

Commissioned the Winter Palace and Smolny Cathedral, expanded the Russian Empire and oversaw The Seven Years' War

Elizabeth Petrovna was the daughter of Peter the Great and his peasant wife, Catherine I, who became Empress of Russia on their marriage. After her father's and mother's death, her infant cousin took the throne with his mother, Anna Leopoldovna, acting as regent. Elizabeth was quick to rectify the situation and seized the throne back from them in a dramatic coup. Having cultivated a close friendship with the Russian guards, she visited a regiment to ask for their help, while wearing a metal breastplate and wielding a silver cross. Together they marched to the palace and arrested the Emperor and his mother. Elizabeth promised on gaining the throne that she would never issue a death sentence, a promise which, unusually for the time, she kept. Russia flourished under her reign. She established universities in Moscow and Saint Petersburg, expanded the empire, led the country in several international wars and commissioned the Winter Palace. Privately, she was a colourful character. Towards the end of her reign she greatly enjoyed Metamorphoses Balls, which she held once a week; attendees were expected to come dressed as the opposite sex. Elizabeth liked to attend dressed as a Cossack or a carpenter. Never married, her great love was supposedly Alexei Razumovsky, a Ukrainian peasant later known as the 'Emperor of the Night'.

'Whom do you want to serve: me, your natural sovereign, or those who have stolen my inheritance?'

Catherine the Great

Dates: 1729–96
Country of origin: Russia

Expanded the Russian Empire, establishing it as a Western power, and was a patron of the arts and education

A formidable ruler, Empress Catherine II, or Catherine the Great, helmed one of Russia's golden ages. Born Princess Sophie in the then-kingdom of Prussia, she came to Russia to marry the heir to the throne, Peter III. She arrived with zeal for learning Russian ways, converting to Orthodoxy and taking the Orthodox name Catherine in 1774. Her energy and enthusiasm for Russia impressed the Russian nobility, especially compared to her sickly and ill-tempered husband, whom she deposed soon after he came to power. She is remembered as having been one of the great rulers of Russia, overseeing the Russian Enlightenment, expanding the Russian Empire through both warfare and diplomacy, and reforming Russia's administration. She was also a writer and corresponded with greats, such as Diderot and Voltaire.

'You philosophers are lucky men. You write on paper and paper is patient. Unfortunate Empress that I am, I write on the susceptible skins of living beings.'

Caroline Herschel

Dates: 1750–1848
Country of origin: Germany

> *Discovered eight comets, 16 nebulae and was made an honorary fellow of the English Royal Astronomical Society*

Caroline and two of her brothers, Alexander and William, moved to England to forge careers as musicians but they soon turned their eyes to the skies. William resolved to make his own telescope and oversaw the project with Alexander and Caroline. Within eight years he had discovered a new planet. Soon after, Caroline discovered her own comet with her small telescope dubbed 'skysweeper'. The first woman in the world to discover a comet, she sent ripples through English society. People were eager to meet the 'Comet Huntress'. She continued to make discoveries throughout her life, totalling eight comets and 16 nebulae; she became the first woman in England to hold a government position and the joint first woman to be admitted to the Royal Astronomical Society.

'I did not go to rest till I had wrote to Dr Blagden and Mr Aubert to announce the comet.'

Mary Wollstonecraft

Dates: 1759–97
Country of origin: England

An original Western feminist philosopher and author of *A Vindication of the Rights of Woman*

Mary was an activist all her life; she had worked as a lady's companion in her teenage years and published *Thoughts on the Education of Daughters* at 28. In it she protested against the lack of educational opportunities for women. Later, she travelled around France and wrote *A Vindication of the Rights of Men*, exploring the equality she hoped would come from the French Revolution. She expanded on this in her most famous work *A Vindication of the Rights of Woman*, which laid the foundations for the first wave of Western feminism. Mary argued for the importance of women in a functioning society and their potential to achieve if they were to receive an education. In her lifetime, Mary forged her own place in society: she supported herself by tutoring aristocratic girls, eventually setting up a school for girls, lived in the notoriously dangerous revolutionary France, took artist Henry Fuseli as a lover, had a child out of wedlock with American businessman Gilbert Imlay and married anarchist William Godwin, with whom she had a second child, author Mary Shelley (p.45).

Wang Zhenyi

Dates: 1768–97
Country of origin: China

Author of at least 12 books, including explorations of mathematical theorems, astronomy and original poetry

Wang Zhenyi was a largely self-taught mathematician and astronomer, who lived during the Qing Dynasty. She travelled widely in her youth, expanding her skill set far beyond the expectations of a woman at the time. In addition to teaching herself poetry, mathematics and astronomy, she learned martial arts and horse riding from the wife of a Mongolian general. Although she did not originate much new mathematical thinking herself, Wang Zhenyi wrote extensively on existing theorems. She explored famous mathematical texts, rewriting them in simpler language so others were better able to access this knowledge. Unusually for the time, Wang Zhenyi also taught male students.

'It's made to believe,
Women are the same as Men;
Are you not convinced,
Daughters can also be heroic?'

Ching Shih

Dates: 1775–1844
Country of origin: China

> Leader of the largest pirate fleet in history, and undefeated by the British, Portuguese and Chinese navies

In an age when most pirates were men who led short lives with grisly ends, Ching Shih stands out as a female pirate with a successful career. In her lifetime she led the largest pirate fleet in history, known as the Red Flag Fleet, which was rumoured to number 70,000 men. (In comparison, the infamous Blackbeard commanded four ships containing around 300 men.) Her rules were strict and her punishments severe; for example, any sailor found guilty of raping a female captive was beheaded. She battled and won against the mighty Portuguese and British navies, even holding members of the powerful East India Trading Company captive. Eventually, presumably tiring of piratical life, she accepted the Qing Imperial Government's offer of money in exchange for retirement. She was reputed to then live a comfortable life as a brothel madam, dying at the ripe old age of 69.

'We shall see how you prove yourselves under the hand of a woman.'

I hate to hear you talk about all women as if they were fine ladies instead of rational creatures. None of us want to be in calm waters all our lives.

JANE AUSTEN

1775–1817

English writer famous for her wit and satirical ability, and author of some of the most famous novels in the English language, including the oft-adapted *Pride and Prejudice*.

> **I am not bound to
> give reasons for what
> I do to anybody.**

LADY HESTER STANHOPE

1776–1839

Society hostess, explorer of
the Middle East and surrounding
areas and early archaeologist.

Mary Shelley

Dates: 1797–1851
Country of origin: England

Author of Frankenstein, *an early science fiction novel*

Mary Shelley was the daughter of Mary Wollstonecraft (p.40) and anarchist and mathematician William Godwin. She ran away from home aged 17 with poet Percy Bysshe Shelley, to whom she had lost her virginity on her mother's grave (and who was rumoured to have had an affair with her half-sister). It was two years later that the Shelleys and their friend Lord Byron challenged each other to write scary stories. Both Percy Bysshe Shelley and Lord Byron were recognised poets in the Romantic movement at the time, so it seemed they had the advantage. Still, aged only 19, Mary wrote the text that would become *Frankenstein*, one of the earliest science fiction texts. It was received well at the time and has only grown in popularity since. Its themes of technology, identity and morality still resonate, and the novel's influence is felt in both modern-day science fiction and horror, proving Frankenstein's creature to be one of the world's most enduring pop culture monsters.

'My dreams were all my own; I accounted for them to nobody; they were my refuge when annoyed – my dearest pleasure when free.'

If a single word can change the course of history, another word, in darkness, can defeat the storm.

MANUELA SÁENZ

1797–1856

Peruvian revolutionary and spy, who worked to liberate Venezuela, Bolivia, Colombia, Ecuador and Peru from Spanish rule.

Mary Anning

Dates: 1799–1847
Country of origin: England

Discovered the first complete plesiosaur skeleton and the first ichthyosaur skeleton and made several other important scientific discoveries

Mary Anning lived on the Jurassic Coast of England and collected fossils with her family from a young age, selling them to tourists. When she was 12, she and her brother discovered a complete ichthyosaur skeleton. It was sold as a 'fossilised crocodile skeleton' but was later recognised as the first discovery of its kind. After her father died, Mary helmed the family business of selling fossils and continued to make important discoveries; her personal collection grew and became renowned. Although she was never truly accepted in the palaeontological community of the time, her contributions to science were posthumously recognised.

'[The icythyosaur skeleton] is large and heavy, but one thing I may venture to assure you it is the first and only one discovered in Europe.'

Fanny Mendelssohn

Dates: 1805–47
Country of origin: Germany

Composed over 450 works, many published under her brother Felix's name

Fanny Mendelssohn and her brother Felix both learned music, including instruction on the piano and composition. In their youths, they were marked by their teachers as especially talented. Fanny wasn't encouraged by her family to consider music as a career and she initially published her work under her brother's name, while Felix rose to prominence as a Romantic composer and performer. Their works achieved contemporary acclaim and Felix gave credit where he was able: Queen Victoria told Felix her favourite of his works was 'Italien', which he awkwardly confessed was by Fanny. Fanny died young from a stroke, shortly after publishing her first works under her own name. Music historians continue to untangle which of Felix's attributed works belong to Fanny and her renown as a composer is growing steadily.

'I have been composing a good deal lately, and have called my piano pieces after the names of my favourite haunts… They will form a delightful souvenir, a kind of second diary.'

Ada Lovelace

Dates: 1815–52
Country of origin: Germany

> Helped develop Charles Babbage's 'Analytical Engine', published the first computer algorithm, considered the first computer programmer

Ada Lovelace was the daughter of libertine Romantic poet Lord Byron and his wife Lady Byron. Appalled at the life her wild husband had lived, Lady Byron encouraged Ada to develop an interest in mathematics in an attempt to steer her from her father's path. Ada flourished under the tutelage of polymath Mary Somerville and, through her, met Charles Babbage. It was her work on Babbage's Analytical Engine (an early computer) that cemented her place in history. Ada published a translation of a paper written on the Engine and included her own notes. Among them was an algorithm that would run the machine – the first of its kind – and the first published consideration that a computer might be used for things other than mere calculation. Ada later gained the nickname 'the Enchantress of Numbers' for her work with Babbage.

LIFE APPEARS TO ME TOO SHORT TO BE SPENT IN NURSING ANIMOSITY, OR REGISTERING WRONGS.

CHARLOTTE BRONTË

1816–55

English author, one of the famous Brontë sisters.

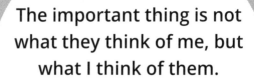

The important thing is not what they think of me, but what I think of them.

QUEEN VICTORIA

1819–1901

Long-reigning English monarch who presided over the British Empire.

Harriet Tubman

Dates: *c.*1820–1913
Country of origin: America

Ran a portion of the Underground Railroad and assisted escaped slaves

Harriet Tubman's life is one built from amazing feats, each an act of bravery that would alone mark any life as extraordinary. She escaped from slavery with her two brothers, only to return and help free her niece and her niece's husband and children. For the following years, Harriet ran a leg of the Underground Railroad, undertaking at least seven more rescues. When the American Civil War broke out she joined as a cook and a nurse for the United States Army, later running missions as a spy and, eventually, a soldier. She was the first woman to lead an assault in the war, freeing more than 750 slaves in the Combahee River Raid. Later in life she joined the women's suffrage movement, campaigning for the emancipation of women.

'I had reasoned this out in my mind: there was one of two things I had a right to, liberty, or death; if I could not have one, I would have the other.'

I never lose an opportunity of urging a practical beginning, however small, for it is wonderful how often in such matters the mustard-seed germinates and roots itself.

FLORENCE NIGHTINGALE

1820–1910

Victorian nurse, pioneer of hospital hygiene and first admitted female member to the Royal Statistical Society. Known as 'The Lady with the Lamp'.

I declare to you that woman must not depend upon the protection of man, but must be taught to protect herself, and there I take my stand.

SUSAN B. ANTHONY

1820–1906

American anti-slavery and women's rights activist who helped women achieve suffrage in several states.

I AM NOT AFRAID TO LIVE, TO CHASE AFTER DREAMS.

ANITA GARIBALDI

1821–49

Brazilian revolutionary who fought against Brazilian, Argentine and Austrian imperial forces at the side of her husband Giuseppe Garibaldi.

There must be a
battle, a brave boisterous
battle, with pennants waving
and cannon roaring before there
can be peaceful treaties and
enthusiastic shaking of hands.

MARY ELIZABETH BRADDON

1835–1915

Popular English novelist and
editor whose work includes
Lady Audley's Secret.

Elizabeth Garrett Anderson

Dates: 1836–1917
Country of origin: England

> First British woman to qualify as a doctor in Europe, and
> first female mayor in Britain

Although Elizabeth Garrett Anderson faced many obstacles in her quest to become a doctor – including the medical students of the college she was attending giving a presentation arguing for her to be expelled from the institute (she was) – she never gave up. She exploited a loophole in the rules of the Society of Apothecaries and qualified as a medical practitioner with them (whereupon they swiftly changed their rules to bar women). Refused employment by other practices, she opened her own and grew it over several years. Eventually she gained membership to the prestigious British Medical Association (who also promptly voted to disallow any further women). Among her later achievements was her election as Mayor of Aldeburgh; she was the first woman to hold such a position in England.

*'The first thing women must learn is to dress like
ladies and behave like gentlemen.'*

Berthe Morisot

Dates: 1841–95
Country of origin: France

Influential artist and an originator of Impressionism

Impressionism developed as an artistic movement in nineteenth century Paris, during a tumultuous period of war and rebuilding. Initially rejected by the art establishment, it came to be a movement of cutting-edge modernity. Berthe's work was featured in the first (commercially unsuccessful) Impressionist exhibition, alongside other originators of the style. Berthe went on to exhibit in six of the seven exhibitions staged by the artists considered to be the founders of Impressionism. Although, as a woman, Berthe was barred from Parisian café culture – which heavily informed both the style and content of Impressionist art – she still explored scenes of modern life through her paintings. This was groundbreaking in an art scene largely formed by portraits, interpretations of Biblical scenes and idealised rural landscapes. Although few of the Impressionists, including Berthe, were financially successful in their lifetime, at the time of her death she had outsold Monet, Renoir and Sisley.

'My ambition is limited to capturing something transient.'

> Love largely and hate nothing. Hold no aim that does not chord with universal good.

ELLA WHEELER WILCOX

1850–1919

Popular American author and poet, originator of the phrase 'laugh and the world laughs with you'.

Courage! Victory is ours!

TAYTU BETUL

1851–1918

Empress of Ethiopia, key in repelling the
invading forces of Italy and negotiating
peace terms after her victory.

Ida B. Wells

Dates: 1862–1931
Country of origin: America

Civil rights activist, who led an anti-lynching campaign

Ida B. Wells was born into slavery and freed in her teens. Her first profession was as a teacher, but she also became involved in civil rights activism when, aged 22, she sued a railway company for attempting to move her to a smoking carriage despite her possession of a first-class ticket. She won, although the decision was later reversed, and she started writing editorials protesting Jim Crow laws (US laws enforcing racial segregation). Ida came to national attention when she wrote a series of editorials railing against lynchings; she travelled around Southern America at great danger to herself to report on the atrocities taking place there. Ida continued to fight for civil rights and women's suffrage throughout her life, eventually co-founding the National Association for the Advancement of Colored People (NAACP), which is still active today.

*'The way to right wrongs is to turn
the light of truth upon them.'*

Madam C. J. Walker

Dates: 1867–1919
Country of origin: America

Civil rights activist and the first self-made female millionaire in America

The first of her family born into freedom, Madam Walker worked at menial jobs for decades until, in her thirties, she became a salesperson for Malones, a company specialising in hair-care products for women of colour. Aided by her barber brothers, Madam Walker developed her own line of products in this market and went into business for herself. Starting with door-to-door sales, she grew her business until she employed nearly 20,000 women. Madam Walker became not only the first black American millionaire but the first self-made female American millionaire in history.

'I have built my own factory on my own ground.'

I INTEND TO CREATE A
BOX WITHOUT WALLS.
A BOX WITHOUT WALLS
IS ONE THAT ALLOWS
ITS OCCUPANTS TO
TREAD WHEREVER THEIR
FEET MIGHT LEAD AND
STRETCH THEIR ARMS AS
WIDE AS THEY WISH.

TOSHIKO KISHIDA

1863–1901

From her famous 'Daughters in Boxes'
speech about the limits placed on
women in Japanese society.

Marie Curie

Dates: 1867–1934
Country of origin: Poland

Two-time Nobel Prize winner, who discovered the elements polonium and radium

Marie Curie blazed a trail in science. She was the first woman to win a Nobel Prize, for her pioneering research in the field of radiology. When she won her second Nobel Prize for her discovery of the two elements polonium and radium, she became the second – and, to-date, only female – scientist to win a Nobel Prize in two categories. Marie's path to learning hadn't been smooth. Women weren't allowed to attend university in her native Poland and she had to attend secret classes until she could escape to Paris and enrol there. The Nobel committee even thought about not honouring her for the first Nobel Prize she was nominated for, until her husband – who had worked on the same project and was also a nominee – discovered this and complained. Marie's work in radiology

– a field she herself named – shaped modern history. Her discovery of and research into the radioactivity of radium are the foundations that cancer treatment is built on. Sadly, Marie died from exposure to radiation, having frequently carried samples of radium on her person and unknowingly contaminated her household items with it.

'Nothing in life is to be feared, it is only to be understood. Now is the time to understand more, so that we may fear less.'

Isabelle Eberhardt

Dates: 1877–1904
Country of origin: Switzerland

Author of several short stories and books, and an anti-colonialist activist

Isabelle Eberhardt's life was short and wildly unconventional for the time. She spent her childhood travelling with her family, often preferring to wear boys' clothes, which was encouraged by her anarchist, atheist father. She became interested in North Africa and moved to Algiers on the encouragement of a photographer friend. While there, she converted to Islam and dressed as a man. Towards the end of her life she exclusively dressed in men's clothing, was known by the masculine name Si Mahmoud Saadi and referred to herself using both masculine and feminine pronouns. A friend commented that Isabelle 'drank more than a Legionnaire, smoked more kief than a hashish addict and made love for the love of making love'. She left Algiers and travelled around, writing novels which were only posthumously successful and falling in and out of love, sometimes being ordered to leave towns by the incumbent regime on suspicion of being a spy. Another friend referred to her as a 'rebel', admiring how she existed 'outside all prejudice, all enslavement, all cliché, and who passes through life as liberated as a bird in space, what a treat!'

Women's great acts and endless sacrifices do not change men's views of women. Through their arrogance, men refuse to see the capabilities of women.

HUDA SHAARAWI

1879–1947

Pioneering Egyptian feminist, founder of the Egyptian Feminist Union.

Virginia Woolf

Dates: 1882–1941
Country of origin: England

Celebrated author of novels, non-fiction essays and reviews, and one of the founding members of the Bloomsbury Set

Virginia Woolf was already a successful author when she published the essay *A Room of One's Own* – the influential feminist tract that would inspire many women. In it she explores the necessity of female financial independence if women are to create works of art. The Bloomsbury Set, of which she was a founding member (although it was never an organisation), was a group of famed artists, writers and thinkers, such as economist John Maynard Keynes and critic Lytton Strachey. Virginia's own books, popular in her lifetime, are now considered modernist masterpieces and are still influential today. Works such as *Orlando*, written as a tribute to her lover Vita Sackville-West, have been adapted into countless plays and films. With her husband, Leonard Woolf, she also founded the Hogarth Press which still exists today.

'A woman must have money and a room of her own if she is to write fiction.'

> **A dame that knows the ropes isn't likely to get tied up.**

MAE WEST

1893–1980

American actress, playwright and script writer, entrepreneur and famous wit.

Bessie Coleman

Dates: 1892–1926
Country of origin: USA

> *Pilot, stunt flier and first African-American woman to hold a pilot's licence*

Bessie was 24 and working as a manicurist in Chicago when she decided she wanted to train as a pilot. She took a second job to pay for her training, but was rejected from American flight schools on the grounds of being both a woman and African-American. Undeterred, she found a sponsor called Jesse Binga, who enabled her to learn French and then to travel to Paris to earn her pilot's licence. Despite becoming a media sensation on her return to the USA, she soon realised she would need to train as a stunt pilot to sustain a living as an aviator. Bessie returned to France and then travelled to the Netherlands and Germany to bolster her training. Billed as 'the world's greatest woman flier', her dramatic and flamboyant acts included performing figures of eight, loop-the-loops and swoops to near-ground level. She dreamed of opening a school for African-American aviators but sadly passed away aged 34 when her plane crashed. However, her legacy lives on, and she remains an inspiration to women everywhere who wish to pursue a career in aviation.

'The air is the only place free from prejudices.'

Freya Stark

Dates: 1893–1993
Country of origin: Italy

Pioneering female explorer, who located the Valley of the Assassins in Iran, and author of over 24 travel books

By the time she was recruited to work for the British Ministry of Information during World War Two, Freya Stark had already undertaken dangerous treks through parts of Iran, producing work that won her the Founder's Gold Medal from the Royal Geographical Society. The areas she travelled, including Iran, Syria, Lebanon and Iraq, had barely been visited by male Western travellers, let alone a woman. During the war, Freya produced pro-British propaganda in Palestine for the MOI. She continued to travel tirelessly for most of her life, writing richly historical travel narratives about Turkey, Afghanistan and others, and was eventually awarded a damehood for her services to travel writing.

> *'To awaken quite alone in a strange town is one of the most pleasant sensations in the world. You are surrounded by adventure.'*

Edith Head

Dates: 1897–1981
Country of origin: USA

Eight-time Oscar winner for best costume design

Edith Head was hired as a studio costume designer in 1924 with little experience – she later admitted that her first portfolio consisted of designs 'borrowed' from her fellow students. Even so, Edith excelled in this role and her designs caused a stir even early in her career. Her work on Mae West's 1933 film *She Done Him Wrong* inspired fashions for women around the world upon release. Soon she was heading up the costume design on most Paramount Studios films. She was so popular that actresses such as Barbara Stanwyck had the stipulation written into their studio contracts that they would work only with her. Edith was responsible for creating many iconic film looks, including Grace Kelly's in *Rear Window* (Edith would work with director Hitchcock 11 times in her career) and Gloria Swanson's in *Sunset Boulevard*. The Oscars category for best costume design was created in 1949 and Edith was immediately nominated, winning the following year. She would go on to be nominated a total of 35 times and win eight, holding the records for both the most Oscar nominations and the most wins by a woman.

Women, like men, should try to do the impossible. And when they fail, their failure should be a challenge to others.

AMELIA EARHART

1897–1939

Record-setting American aviator who found fame after becoming the first woman to fly across the Atlantic Ocean.

WE LIVE IN THE PRESENT, WE DREAM OF THE FUTURE, BUT WE LEARN ETERNAL TRUTHS FROM THE PAST.

SOONG MEI-LING

1898–2003

First Lady of the Republic of China,
influential politician and one of the
politically-active Soong Sisters.

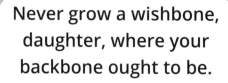

Never grow a wishbone,
daughter, where your
backbone ought to be.

CLEMENTINE PADDLEFORD

1898–1967

Nationally syndicated American food
writer. She was also a pilot and flew herself
to many restaurants and eateries around
the country for her articles.

> **Happiness is to take up the struggle in the midst of the raging storm.**

DING LING

1904–86

Celebrated Chinese writer whose work scrutinised gender roles in the Maoist regime, and author of over 300 works.

Barbara Hepworth

Dates: 1903–75
Country of origin: England

Influential Modernist sculptor, who is among Britain's greatest artists

When Barbara Hepworth created her 1931 sculptural work *Pierced Form* – an abstract shape with a hole through it – Henry Moore declared the following year was 'the year of the hole'. A hole or empty space in the sculptural form became a hallmark of Barbara's Modernist style, allowing a new dimension through which onlookers could experience her work. She was one of the most respected artists of the mid-twentieth century and her work can be found in museums and galleries around the world. Among her most famous pieces is a large bronze sculpture titled *Single Form*, which was commissioned by the United Nations and is currently placed outside their New York headquarters. Appointed a dame for her artistic contribution, she influenced generations of artists and is one of the most noted figures of the Modernist movement.

'You can't look at a sculpture if you are going to stand stiff as a ram rod and stare at it, with a sculpture you must walk around it, bend toward it, touch it and walk away from it.'

I'm not intimidated by anyone. Everyone is made with two arms, two legs, a stomach and a head. Just think about that.

JOSEPHINE BAKER

1906–75

American-French entertainer who was an international sensation, the first black American to star in an international motion picture, an Allied World War Two spy and civil rights activist.

Grace Hopper

Dates: 1906–92
Country of origin: USA

Pioneer of machine-independent programming languages and dubbed the 'grandmother' of COBOL

Grace Hopper was teaching at the prestigious Vassar College and held a PhD in mathematics when, aged 34, she attempted to enlist in the US Navy. Despite the fact that World War Two was raging at the time, she was rejected for her age and size. Undeterred, she joined the Navy Reserves. There she was assigned to the Mark I computer programming department. After the war she joined the team developing UNIVAC, the first computer to market in the United States. It was while developing UNIVAC I that Grace recommended building a programming language based on English instead of the binary code that was already being used. It took three years for her suggestion to be taken seriously, as people did not think computers would be able to understand English, but she eventually developed a language that did so. A team, with the aid of Grace, developed this into COBOL, a computer language still being used in businesses around the world today.

Frida Kahlo

Dates: 1907–54
Country of origin: Mexico

> *Influential Surrealist artist, who created over 200 works*

Frida was studying medicine at the prestigious Escuela Nacional Preparatoria when she was involved in a serious accident while travelling by bus. She had over thirty surgeries and the pain and injury dogged her for the rest of her life. While she was recovering, bedridden, she turned to painting to pass the time. Frida's work was rich in folk imagery from her native Mexico, and it explored her personal experiences, many of which featured variations of self-portraiture. In her lifetime she rejected the label of 'Surrealist artist', though the father of Surrealism, André Breton, considered her one. Frida was politically active, giving Leon Trotsky shelter when he was expelled from Russia by the Stalinist regime (she is alleged to have had an affair with him). She was also feted in her lifetime;

the Louvre acquired her work, *Self-Portrait: The Frame,* in 1939, which made her the first twentieth-century Mexican artist to be collected by the renowned museum. Not even her famous muralist husband, Diego Rivera, had achieved that. Frida is still famed worldwide today and is considered a feminist and South American hero.

'I never painted dreams. I painted my own reality.'

WE ARE WOMEN, WE ARE WORKERS, WE STAND TOGETHER.

LILLIAN NGOYI

1911–80
South African politician and
anti-apartheid activist.

Marie-Madeleine Fourcade

Dates: 1909–89
Country of origin: France

Led the French resistance group 'Alliance' during World War Two and helped found Charles de Gaulle's Union for the New Republic Party

Marie-Madeleine Fourcade started her resistance efforts writing for the magazine *L'ordre National*, which reported on Hitler's actions from inside occupied France. The editor, Georges Loustaunau-Lacau, also ran the 3,000-strong network of resistance agents known as 'Alliance'. Finding the two tasks overwhelming, he asked Marie-Madeleine to head Alliance and, after some resistance, she agreed. She recruited agents across Vichy, France, and gathered knowledge that informed the Allied forces on weapons, arsenals and troop movements via detailed maps (these were used in planning D-Day). By 1943 she was considered important enough that the British government smuggled her out of France, but she returned and was captured by the occupying German forces. Not only did she manage to escape by squeezing out of her cell window, but she also warned an important spy in her network that he was about to be arrested. She continued her work until the end of the war, becoming a member of the European Parliament in peacetime.

Dorothy Hodgkin

Dates: 1910–94
Country of origin: England

Nobel Prize winner in chemistry, pioneer in the field of X-ray technology and the first woman to receive the Copley Medal

Dorothy Hodgkin's work on determining the structures of molecules is part of the essential groundwork that modern-day structural biology is built upon. While studying the B12 vitamin, Dorothy realised that she could use X-ray technology to determine its molecular structure, which then allowed scientists to learn more about how B12 functioned and how it could be used to make medicines or materials. Her discovery earned her a Nobel Prize in chemistry; she was only the third woman to earn this award. However, this was not her only major achievement. Dorothy's tireless – and ultimately successful – efforts to discern the complex structure of insulin led to breakthroughs in treatments for diabetes. Later, for outstanding contributions to science, Dorothy was granted the prestigious Copley Medal and, as of July 2018, remains the only woman to ever receive it.

'I was captured for life by chemistry and by crystals.'

You can't win them all – but you can try.

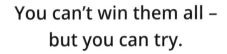

BABE DIDRIKSON ZAHARIAS

1911–56

All-star American athlete who has two gold Olympic medals in athletics and ten Ladies Professional Golf Association championship wins among her many sporting achievements.

> In science, all facts, no matter how trivial or banal, enjoy democratic equality.

MARY McCARTHY

1912–89
American novelist and political activist.

Each person must
live their life as a model
for others.

ROSA PARKS

1913–2005
American civil rights activist who, among
many other acts, refused to
give up her seat for a white man.

Hedy Lamarr

Dates: 1914–2000
Country of origin: Austria

Invented a radio device that became the foundation for Bluetooth and Wi-Fi, and starred in several Hollywood films

The early years of Hedy Lamarr's life read like a plot from an Old Hollywood melodrama: after her father died young, leaving the family destitute, Hedy took a part in an avant-garde film called *Ecstasy*, in which she appeared naked and in the throes of passion, which led to her reputation in Europe as 'the Ecstasy girl'. Hedy married a much older man, who forced her into the life of a society hostess for his Fascist friends. She escaped from this controlling relationship and went to Hollywood, where she built a career for herself as a glamorous movie star. For a while her career flourished but she sank into obscurity until, during the seventies, it emerged that Hedy had filed a patent for a device that had been used to create untraceable missiles. This device went on to be the foundation for 'spread spectrum' communication technology, which is the very thing that Bluetooth and Wi-Fi work by.

'All creative people want to do the unexpected.'

Sister Rosetta Tharpe

Dates: 1915–73
Country of origin: USA

> Blues pioneer and inspiration to artists such as Chuck Berry, Johnny Cash and Elvis Presley

Sister Rosetta Tharpe is largely forgotten by modern rock 'n' roll fans, although that isn't due to the lack of success in her time. She was the first gospel singer to be signed to the influential Decca Records, one of the first black musicians to play at the Cotton Club and, for a while, the most commercially successful gospel artist in the USA. Although she considered herself a gospel artist, her guitar strumming, singing and stage presence can all be seen to foreshadow the rock 'n' roll style. It would almost be quicker to list the artists who haven't credited her as an inspiration. Little Richard, Chuck Berry, Elvis Presley, Johnny Cash, Jerry Lee Lewis, Aretha Franklin, Isaac Hayes, Tina Turner and George Melly have all named her as an influential figure in their successful careers. Luckily, recognition of Sister Rosetta Tharpe's impact is growing and in 2017 she was admitted into the Rock and Roll Hall of Fame.

> *'All this new stuff they call rock 'n' roll, why, I've been playing that for years now.'*

FORGIVENESS IS A VIRTUE OF THE BRAVE.

INDIRA GANDHI

1917–84

India's first and, to-date,
only female prime minister.

Katherine Johnson

Dates: 1918–present
Country of origin: USA

Mathematician for NASA, who calculated the trajectory for Apollo 11, and co-author of 26 scientific papers

Katherine Johnson started her career as a mathematician for the National Advisory Committee for Aeronautics (NACA). The all-male, all-white flight research team was so impressed with her work that she stayed on when the committee was absorbed into NASA. There she worked as an aerospace technologist, calculating trajectories for nearly every significant space travel project NASA were running, including the route for the space flight of the first American in space. When NASA first used electronic computers to calculate a mission – in which John Glenn would orbit the Earth – the astronaut refused to fly until Katherine confirmed the course. In 1969 she was on the team that landed Apollo 11 on the moon. She continued to work at NASA until her retirement in 1986, winning the Presidential Medal of Freedom in 2015.

'If you like what you're doing, you will do well.'

One newspaperman wrote that I was too old to run, that I should stay at home and take care of my children. When I got to London, I pointed my finger at him and I said, 'I show you.'

FANNY BLANKERS-KOEN

1918–2004

Record-setting Dutch athlete who won four gold medals at the 1948 Olympics.

> I know that like every woman of the people, I have more strength than I appear to have.

EVA PERÓN

1919–1952

Born into poverty, she passionately lobbied for pro-labour rights and women's suffrage during her time as First Lady of Argentina.

They thought that if I were arrested the revolution would lose its force. They didn't realise that the revolution was carried on by the whole people, not only me.

NGUYỄN THỊ ĐỊNH

1920–1992

Commander of an all-female contingent of the Vietnamese People's Army known as 'The Long-haired Army' and prominent Vietnamese politician.

Mirabal sisters

Dates: *c.*1924–60
Country of origin: Dominican Republic

Actively opposed the Dominican dictator Rafael Trujillo

The Mirabal sisters consisted of Patria, Dedé, María Teresa and Minerva, although Dedé was not active in the resistance movement. After experiencing the oppression and atrocity committed by their country's dictator, Rafael Trujillo, they formed a resistance movement named the Fourteenth of June Movement. The sisters' alias was 'Las Mariposas' – The Butterflies – and they worked to create dissent against the Trujillo regime. They distributed pamphlets and collected arms for the revolution to come. In 1960 the group unsuccessfully attempted to assassinate Trujillo and were exposed and thrown in jail. The sisters were 'released' but then killed by the secret police a short while later. Their deaths enraged the Dominican people and, only six months after, Trujillo was assassinated. The Mirabal sisters continue to be national heroes; most Dominican towns bear their name on their streets and their schools, and the United Nations designated the International Day for the Elimination of Violence Against Women in their honour.

The Night Witches

Dates: Assorted, *c.*1940s
Country of origin: USSR

A feared all-female Soviet volunteer unit of military aviators

Although women served in more active roles in Russia during World War Two than in any other country, they still found themselves blocked from the more dangerous areas of combat. Marina Raskova, already a famous aviator in Russia, used her personal connection with Russian leader Stalin to persuade him to allow her to form three all-female military aviation units. One of them, the 588th Night Bomber Regiment, came to be known as the Night Witches. By the close of the war, many women in the regiment had flown an estimated 800 missions, and their accuracy was so feared that the German military promised an Iron Cross to every pilot who shot a Night Witch down. The commander of the regiment, Yevdokia Bershanskaya, was awarded the Order of the Red Banner and 23 others were made Heroes of Russia for their war efforts.

*'What we did have were clever,
educated, very talented girls.'*
Nadezhda Popova, Night Witch, commenting on the German
rumours that the Night Witches were so good that they must
have been issued drugs to give them night vision.

WE ENCOUNTER MANY DEFEATS, BUT MUST NEVER BE <u>DEFEATED</u>.

MAYA ANGELOU

1928–2014

American poet, diarist and civil rights activist whose 1969 memoir *I Know Why the Caged Bird Sings* is considered one of the defining modern works of the genre.

Toni Morrison

Dates: 1931–present
Country of origin: USA

Winner of the Nobel Prize for Literature and the Pulitzer Prize, and awarded the US Presidential Medal of Freedom

Toni Morrison grew up in racially segregated America. As an editor in New York, she worked to create a space for black authors and readers, publishing anthologies by black writers and furthering the careers of talented individuals, such as Angela Davis. It was her own writing, though, that blazed a path through the overwhelmingly white landscape of twentieth-century Western literature. Her novel *Beloved* won her the Pulitzer Prize for fiction in 1985 and its ensuing trilogy was awarded the Nobel Prize for Literature in 1993. Toni has been vocal about the injustices faced by African-Americans in US society; her work engages with the reality of many black lives and she has been outspoken on many issues, most recently writing the essay 'Mourning for Whiteness' on the rise of the far right in America and the election of Donald Trump.

'I thought, "Wait a minute, there's no book in there about me!" So if I wanted to read it, I would probably have to write it.'

Every individual matters.
Every individual has a role
to play. Every individual
makes a difference.

JANE GOODALL

1934–present

English conservationist and anthropologist,
named a UN Messenger of Peace. Known
for her work researching chimpanzee
social life, she is considered the world's
foremost chimpanzee expert.

Sylvia Earle

Dates: 1935–present
Country of origin: USA

First female chief scientist of the US National Oceanic and Atmospheric Administration, explorer-in-residence for National Geographic and Time magazine's first Hero for the Planet

Sylvia Earle grew up in a nature-loving family in New Jersey. She had always loved wildlife, but it was her fascination with the sea that set her on the path to a long and successful career. By 1966, she had received her doctorate in phycology from Duke University, North Carolina, with her pioneering research into seaweed and algae. In 1970 she participated in a project called Tektite II, which involved living underwater for two weeks and leading an all-female team named Mission 6; she has lived underwater a total of ten times in her lifetime. Sylvia once held the record for the deepest solo dive, as she walked along the ocean floor in a mechanised diving suit built to withstand the pressures of the deep. She has discovered many new marine species throughout her career, with several named after her. Some call her 'Her Deepness' and 'The Sturgeon General', and she was the founding member of the Ocean Elders, a group dedicated to protecting the oceans of the world. She has pioneered her own 'Mission Blue', whose aim is to create a series of protected marine areas – there are currently nearly 100 of these around the globe.

'That's our gift – to understand that we are a part of nature, not apart [from] it.'

> **A feminist is anyone who recognises the equality and full humanity of women and men.**

GLORIA STEINEM

1934–present

American journalist and social activist who wrote several pieces important to second-wave feminism, including an exposé on life as a Playboy bunny.

Well-behaved women seldom make history.

LAUREL THATCHER ULRICH

1938–present
American historian, who focused
on histories of women.

Valentina Tereshkova

Dates: 1937–present
Country of origin: Russia

The first woman in space

When Valentina Tereshkova was given the opportunity to train to be the first woman in space, she was a 24-year-old textile factory worker and an enthusiastic amateur parachute jumper. It was 1961 and Russia and the US were locked in a space race. Russia was ahead, having fielded the first live animal in orbit – Laika the dog – and the first man in space, Russian hero Yuri Gagarin. Valentina completed her training and, in 1963, became the first woman in space. She orbited for three days and landed safely, despite being sent incorrect landing co-ordinates, which she had to recalculate to avoid going into deep space instead of back to Earth! Valentina was awarded honours around the world, including the highest honour of the USSR, the Hero of the Soviet Union. She never returned to space, although she always wished to; Valentina has said on record that she would like to join a Mars mission.

'Anyone who has spent any time in space will love it for the rest of their lives.'

Wilma Rudolph

Dates: 1940–94
Country of origin: USA

One-time fastest woman in the world, first African-American woman to win three gold medals in one Olympic games, civil rights activist

In 1960 the summer Olympics were broadcast on television for the first time in the US. Sportspeople became stars overnight. One such star was Wilma Rudolph. Wilma hadn't always been the likeliest Olympic candidate – a childhood bout of Polio forced her to wear a leg brace for a while and she had her first child while still in high school – but by 1960 she was at the top of her game. Not only did she set the world record for the 200-metre sprint during the qualifiers, but she also set a new Olympic record during the 200-metre heats, taking gold for that race and for all others she competed in: the 100-metre sprint and the 4 x 100-metre relay. Along with those victories, she became the first African-American woman to win three golds in a single Olympiad, and was dubbed 'the fastest woman in history' and 'The Tornado'. She retired in 1962, still at the top of her game, and became a teacher, coach and civil rights activist.

'The triumph can't be had without the struggle.'

IN A TIME OF DESTRUCTION, CREATE SOMETHING.

MAXINE HONG KINGSTON

1940–present
Chinese-American feminist
author and anti-war activist.

Janis Joplin

Dates: 1943–70
Country of origin: USA

Influential rock musician and pioneering female singer

In 1961 Janis Joplin left her Texas college to hitchhike to San Francisco, where she immersed herself in a drifting hippy lifestyle (this freewheeling personality was something Janis would never truly shake off; she briefly left music at the height of her fame to backpack around Brazil). Her career took off with *Cheap Thrills*, her band Big Brother and the Holding Company's second album. For two years Janis would blaze bright as a wild-haired, wild-voiced and wildly talented singer. Her tracks 'Piece of My Heart' and 'Mercedes-Benz' provided some of the soundtrack to 1960s counterculture. Janis tragically died young of an overdose but left behind a legacy that would inspire generations of musicians to follow.

'Singing is like loving somebody. It's an emotional and physical experience.'

Billie Jean King

Dates: 1943–present
Country of origin: USA

Tennis champion and campaigner for women's rights in the sport

Billie Jean King won 39 Grand Slam titles over the course of her career and is widely considered to be one of the greatest female tennis players of all time. She worked hard to improve conditions for female tennis players, withdrawing from the existing tennis tours and forming her own tournament, The Virginia Slims Circuit, when the existing US tennis federation would not improve appearance fees and prize money to bring women's winnings closer in line with men's. She also founded the Women's Tennis Association, now the principal organising body for women's tennis, and the Women's Sports Foundation, a non-profit organisation dedicated to helping women to get involved in more sport. At the height of her career and her campaign for greater equality in the sport, she famously beat former tennis champion Bobby Riggs in a match dubbed 'Battle of the Sexes'. She also acknowledged a relationship with a woman in 1981, while still playing professionally – a move that was rare for the time and caused her to lose $2 million in sponsorship deals. Later, in 1987, she fell in love with her doubles partner Ilana Kloss, who she is still with today.

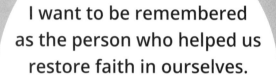

I want to be remembered
as the person who helped us
restore faith in ourselves.

WILMA MANKILLER

1945–2010

Cherokee chief and activist for
indigenous and women's rights.

Marcia Lucas

Dates: 1945–present
Country of origin: USA

Edited Martin Scorsese's Taxi Driver *and* New York, New York, *and won an Oscar for best film editing for* Star Wars

By the time Marcia Lucas came to work on her then-husband George Lucas' new film, *Star Wars*, she had already built a reputation for herself in Hollywood. Her work as assistant editor on *The Graduate* had earned her a recommendation to a young Martin Scorsese, who first hired her to edit his film *Alice Doesn't Live Here Anymore*. He was impressed and kept her on board for his next film, the seminal *Taxi Driver*, for which she earned a BAFTA nomination. Meanwhile, George Lucas had shot *Star Wars* and had it edited by an English editor but he wasn't happy; the cut was stodgy and boring. Marcia agreed to step in and worked against the clock with fellow editor Richard Chew to get it ready for its launch date. It was – it is almost unnecessary to say – a success, and Marcia earned an Oscar for her work. Sadly the Lucases marriage broke up and, after working on *The Return of the Jedi*, Marcia left the film industry for good. However, her legacy lives on in the films for millions of *Star Wars* fans.

If you don't like the road you're walking, start paving another one.

DOLLY PARTON

1946–present

US country singer and businesswoman, who numbers nine Grammy awards among her many achievements.

Katharine Hamnett

Dates: 1947–present
Country of origin: England

Political and ethical fashion pioneer

While most fashion houses remain firmly disengaged with politics, Katharine Hamnett has always embedded her political stance in her designs. She rose to fame with her captioned shirts; among other celebrities, George Michael wore her 'Choose Life' T-shirt in the video for Wham's 'Wake Me Up Before You Go-Go' in 1984. She herself wore a T-shirt captioned '58% don't want Pershing' when meeting then-prime minister, Margaret Thatcher. (Pershing was a type of missile due to be stored in Britain.) Katharine was environmentally conscious before it was fashionable to be so, too. She commissioned an environmental impact study on her own business and was so appalled by the results that she closed her brand and rebuilt it to be an ethical company that minimised its environmental impact, avoided pesticides and didn't use sweatshop factories. Recent designs include the captions 'NHS NOT TRIDENT' and 'CANCEL BREXIT'.

> *'The price of clothes may be low but they
> are paid for with human lives.'*

All adventures, especially into new territory, are scary.

SALLY RIDE

1951–2012

The youngest American astronaut to reach space, the third woman in space and the first LGBT astronaut.

WHEN ANYONE TELLS ME I CAN'T DO ANYTHING, I'M JUST NOT LISTENING ANY MORE.

FLORENCE GRIFFITH JOYNER

1959–98

American athlete and current world record-holder for the 100-metre and 200-metre sprint, dubbed 'The Fastest Woman of All Time'.

Conclusion

You have now read about just some of the greatest women in history. You have seen that women have excelled in every field they have turned their hand to, and among their number include powerful rulers, pioneering scientists and mathematicians, feared warriors, cutting-edge artists and record-breaking sportspeople. Women have fought for – and achieved – so much and, thanks to our wonderful predecessors, we are living in a time where we are closer to equality than ever before. Hopefully you have been inspired by their stories. And yet, even the 50-something-strong list of ladies in this book merely scratches the surface of female achievement through the years. Read on to find further lists of prominent women across different fields, or you can check the reading list to see where you should start if you want to find out more about the awesome women in this book.

More Great Women

More rulers

Sammu-ramat, Queen of Assyria
Cleopatra, Pharaoh of Egypt
Arawelo, Queen of Somalia
Himiko, shamaness-queen of Yamataikoku
Brunhilda of Austrasia, Queen of Austrasia
Wu Zetian, Empress of China
Töregene Khatun, regent of the Mongol Empire
Isabella of Castile, Queen of Castile
Lili'uokalani, Queen of Hawai'i
Maria Leopoldina of Austria, Empress Consort of Brazil

More artists

Johanna Vergouwen, Baroque painter
Sarah Biffen, portrait miniaturist
Harriet Hosmer, Neoclassical sculptor
Marianne North, biologist and botanical artist
Marie Bracquemond, French Impressionist painter
Mary Cassatt, American Impressionist painter
Georgia O'Keeffe, renowned Modernist artist
Gerda Taro, war photographer
Meret Oppenheim, Surrealist artist
Cindy Sherman, American photographer

More explorers

Jeanne Baret, first woman to circumnavigate the globe

Ida Laura Pfeiffer, traveller and writer

Isabella Bird, traveller and writer

Annie Smith Peck, American mountaineer

Mary Kingsley, explorer and science writer

Alexandra David-Neel, explorer and anarchist

Gertrude Bell, explorer and diplomat

Lady Grace Hay Drummond-Hay, first woman to travel the world by air

Carol Beckwith, American photographer

Ellen MacArthur, record-breaking sailor

More pirates

Jeanne de Clisson, French privateer

Malika Fadel ben Salvador, Spanish privateer

Sayyida al Hurra, Moroccan queen and pirate

Christina Anna Skytte, Swedish pirate

Anne Dieu-le-Veut, French pirate

Mary Read, English pirate

Ingela Gathenhielm, Swedish privateer

Anne Bonny, Irish pirate

More spies and revolutionaries

Micaela Bastidas, Peruvian queen and revolutionary leader

Charlotte Corday, French revolutionary spy and assassin

Policarpa Salavarrieta, Colombian anti-colonialist, spy and revolutionary

Melchora Aquino, Filipina revolutionary

Mata Hari, Dutch World War Two spy

Virginia Hall, American World War Two spy

Nancy Wake, World War Two resistance leader and secret agent

Noor Inayat Khan, British Muslim World War Two spy

More writers

Fanny Burney, novelist and playwright

Emily Brontë, novelist

George Eliot, novelist

Beatrix Potter, children's writer and illustrator

Sigrid Undset, winner of the Nobel Prize for Literature

Ursula K. Le Guin, fantasy and sci-fi author

Zadie Smith, contemporary novelist

More poets

Phillis Wheatley, African-American poet

Elizabeth Barrett Browning, poet

Christina Rossetti, poet

Emily Dickinson, poet

H. D., Modernist poet

Dorothy Parker, satirist, wit and poet

Adrienne Rich, feminist poet

Sylvia Plath, poet and novelist

Audre Lorde, womanist poet

Carol Ann Duffy, English Poet Laureate

More warriors

The Trung Sisters, Vietnamese military leaders

Zenobia, Syrian empress

Khawlah bint al-Azwar, Muslim warrior

Aud the Deep Minded, Norse princess

Matilda of Tuscany, ruler of Northern Italy

Khutulun, Asian princess

Black Agnes, Scottish countess

Keumalahayati, Indonesian admiral

Qiu Jin, Chinese revolutionary

More activists

Sojourner Truth, abolitionist
Mary Seacole, nurse
Elizabeth Cady Stanton, American Suffragist
Nellie Bly, American journalist
Lady Abala Bose, social worker and nurse
Sophia Duleep Singh, princess-suffragist
Leslie Feinberg, transgender and gay rights activist
Sylvia Rivera, transgender rights activist
bell hooks, feminist writer

More musicians

Hildegard of Bingen, composer-nun
Amy Beach, American composer
Barbara Strozzi, singer and Baroque composer
Nina Simone, jazz musician and civil rights activist
Grace Slick, singer-songwriter
Aretha Franklin, soul diva
Patti Smith, singer-songwriter
Poly Styrene, punk singer
Kathleen Hanna, riot grrrl movement pioneer
Ani DiFranco, singer songwriter

More sportswomen

Sonja Henie, Norwegian figure skater
Annemarie Moser-Pröll, Austrian skier
Grete Waitz, Norwegian marathon runner
Nadia Comăneci, Romanian gymnast
Jackie Joyner-Kersee, American athlete
Steffi Graf, German tennis player
Serena Williams, American tennis player
Yelena Isinbayeva, Russian pole-vaulter
Tirunesh Dibaba, Ethiopian long-distance athlete

More scientists

Maria Cunitz, Silesian astronomer
Emille du Chatelet, natural scientist
Mary Somerville, astronomer and science writer
Lise Meitner, Austrian-Swedish physicist
Irène Curie-Joliot, Nobel-Prize-winning chemist
Barbara McClintock, Nobel-Prize-winning geneticist
Maria Goeppert Mayer, Nobel-Prize-winning physicist
Rosalind Franklin, instrumental in the discovery of DNA
Xie Xide, Chinese physicist
Sau Lan Wu, instrumental in the discovery of the Higgs-Boson particle

Reading List

Atwood, Kathryn J. ***Women Heroes of World War II: 26 Stories of Espionage, Sabotage, Resistance, and Rescue*** (2011, Chicago Review Press)

Carson, Anne ***If Not, Winter: Fragments of Sappho*** (2003, Virago)

Castor, Helen ***Joan of Arc: A History*** (2015, Faber & Faber)

Cavendish, Margaret ***Sociable Letters*** (2004, Broadview Press)

Cesaretti, Paolo ***Theodora: Empress of Byzantium*** (2005, The Vendome Press)

Clinton, Catherine ***Harriet Tubman: The Road to Freedom*** (2005, Little, Brown and Company)

Cooney, Kara ***The Woman Who Would be King: Hatshepsut's Rise to Power in Ancient Egypt*** (2015, Oneworld Publications)

Copeland, Rebecca and Melek Ortabasi, editors ***The Modern Murasaki: Writing by Women of Meiji Japan*** (2006, Columbia University Press)

Curie, Eve ***Madam Curie*** (2011, Nabu Press)

De Shong Meador, Betty ***Inanna, Lady of Largest Heart: Poems of the Sumerian High Priestess Enheduanna*** (2001, University of Texas Press)

Deakin, Michael A. B. ***Hypatia of Alexandria: Mathematician and Martyr*** (2007, Prometheus Books)

Eberhardt, Isabelle ***The Nomad*** (2003, Interlink Books)

de Erauso, Catalina ***Lieutenant Nun: Memoir of a Basque Transvestite in the New World*** (1997, Beacon Press)

Finch, Anne ***The Poems of Anne, Countess of Winchilsea, from the Original: Edition of 1713 and from Unpublished Manuscripts*** (2012, Forgotten Books)

Garrett Anderson, Louisa ***Elizabeth Garrett Anderson: 1836–1917*** (2016, Cambridge University Press)

de Gournay, Marie ***Apology for the Woman Writing and Other Works*** (2002, University of Chicago Press)

Head, Edith and Paddy Calistro ***Edith Head's Hollywood*** (2009, Angel City Press)

Hepworth, Barbara ***Barbara Hepworth: A Pictorial Autobiography*** (1977, Moonraker Press)

Hingley, Richard and Christina Unwin ***Boudica: Iron Age Warrior Queen*** (2006, Hambledon Continuum)

Keller, Helen ***The Story of My Life*** (1991, Random House USA)

Le Faye, Deirdre ***Jane Austen's Letters*** (2007, OUP Oxford)

Montefiore, Simon Sebag ***The Romanovs: 1613–1918*** (2017, W&N)

Nguyen Thi Dinh ***No Other Roads to Take: The Memoirs of Mrs. Nguyen Thi Dinh*** (1976, A Comstock Book)

van Schurman, Anna Maria *The Learned Maid: or, Whether A Maid May Be a Scholar?* (1659, John Redmayne)

Shelley, Mary *Frankenstein* (2014, Alma Classics)

Shetterly, Margot Lee *Hidden Figures: the Untold Story of the African American Women Who Helped Win the Space Race* (2017, William Collins)

Shikibu, Murasaki *The Diary of Lady Murasaki* (1996, Penguin Classics)

Stark, Freya *The Valleys of the Assassins: and Other Persian Travels* (1991, Arrow Books Ltd)

Weir, Alison *Eleanor of Aquitaine: By the Wrath of God, Queen of England* (2008, Vintage)

Wells, Ida B. and Alfreda M. Duster *Crusade for Justice: The Autobiography of Ida B. Wells* (1991, University of Chicago Press)

Winterburn, Emily *The Quiet Revolution of Caroline Herschel: The Lost Heroine of Astronomy* (2017, The History Press)

Wollstonecraft, Mary *A Vindication of the Rights of Woman* (2004, Penguin Classics)

Woolf, Virginia *A Room of One's Own* (2002, Penguin Classics)

If you're interested in finding out more
about our books, find us on Facebook at
Summersdale Publishers and follow
us on Twitter at **@Summersdale**.

www.summersdale.com